THE MAN ON
CREWE STATION

Also by John Godfrey

Re-playing the Echo
(Rockingham Press)

John Godfrey

THE MAN ON CREWE STATION

Best wishes
John Godfrey
6-9-14

Rockingham Press

Published in 2011 by
The Rockingham Press
11 Musley Lane,
Ware, Herts SG12 7EN
www.rockinghampress.com

Copyright © John Godfrey, 2011

The right of John Godfrey to be identified as the author of this work has been asserted by him in accordance with Section 77 of the Copyright, Designs and Patents Act 1988

British Library Cataloguing-in-Publication Data

A catalogue record for this book
is available from the British Library

ISBN 978-1-904851-40-0

Printed in Great Britain
by the MPG Group

. . . to this day Crewe Junction marks the wildly exciting frontier where the alien South ends and the North . . . begins.

(W. H. Auden: 'I Like it Cold' – an article for *House & Garden* magazine, 1947)

For Sue (still my sternest critic)

*With grateful thanks to Alan and to Siriol
for their help and advice*

and to my parents for giving me a love of words.

ACKNOWLEDGEMENTS

Acknowledgements are due to the editors of the following poetry magazines (some, sadly, now defunct), competition anthologies, and other publications in which some of these poems (or versions of them) first appeared:

Acumen; *Bridport Prize Competition Anthology* 1997; *Chiltern Writers' Group Competiton Anthologies* 2000 and 2001; *Diss Writers Competition Anthology* 2000; *Fatchance*; *The Frogmore Papers*; *The Interpreter's House*; *Kent & Sussex Poetry Society Competition Anthology* 2000; *Newsletter of the Wilfred Owen Association*; *Peterloo Poets Competition Anthologies* 2005 and 2007; *Poetry Ealing*; *Poetry Life*; *Seam*; *Spokes*; *Vision On* (Ver Poets) 2000, 2001, 2002, 2004, and 2006; *Essex Festival Competition Anthology* 2003; and *The White Car* (Ragged Raven Press, 2005).

"A Kind of Alchemy", "Bug", "Last Days", "Life on the Road to Santa Fe", and "Sharpenhoe Clappers" appeared in the pamphlet *Re-playing the Echo* (Rockingham Press, 1995); "Big Sur Café" and "The Permanent Way" appeared in the anthology *In the Company of Poets* (Hearing Eye Press, 2003).

"38 Wetherby Road" won second prize in the Northampton Literature Group Open Poetry Competition 2008; "A Hurrying Stranger" won third prize in the Northampton Literature Group Open Poetry Competition 2003; "A Sudden Surfeit of Squirrels" won first prize in the Northampton Literature Group Open Poetry Competition 2004; "Apprentice" won first prize in the Kick Start Poets Open Poetry Competition 2003; "Big Sur Café" won first prize in the Kent & Sussex Poetry Society Open Poetry Competition 2000; "Cowboy" won third prize in the Ver Poets Open Poetry Competition 2004; "Every Cloud" was a prizewinner in the Peterloo Poets Open Poetry Competition 2007; "Glider" won second prize in the Ver Poets Open Poetry Competition 2001;

"Grandmother's Garden" won second prize in the 12th 'Poetry Life' Open Poetry Competition (1997); "Job Application" came third in the Berkshire Poetry Prize competition 2000; "Like Willow-Pattern" won first prize in the BMI, Wilkins Memorial Poetry Competition 2006; "The man on Crewe station" won first prize in the Peterloo Poets Open Poetry Competition 2005; "Nocturne – Aldeburgh Beach" was second in The Frogmore Prize competition 2007; "The Permanent Way" won first prize in the Chiltern Writers' Group Open Poetry Competition 2000; "Skylark" won second prize in the BMI, Wilkins Memorial Poetry Competition 2006; "Somewhere Close to Hades" won first prize in the Northampton Literature Group Open Poetry Competition 2002; "Time and Place" came fourth in The Bridport Prize competition 1997; "Wall of Death" won second prize in the Kick Start Poets Open Poetry Competition 2002; "We are now approaching…" won first prize in the Northampton Literature Group Open Poetry Competition 2007; and "The White Car" won second prize in the Ragged Raven International Poetry Competition 2005.

A number of the other poems in this collection won lesser prizes or were highly commended or commended in various competitions.

Contents

I

First Draft	15
Wet Day at Lumb Bank	16
Conjurors	17
Stubble-burning	18
A Hurrying Stranger	19
Present Tense, Future Imperfect	20
Time and Place	21
Telephone Man	22
A Sudden Surfeit of Squirrels	23
Every Cloud	24
Bug	26
Skylark	27
Glider	28
Dawn by Numbers	29
Wall of Death	30
Nocturne – Aldeburgh Beach	31
The Devil's Apprentice	32
Job Application	33
The man on Crewe station	34

II

Late Honeymoon	39
"We are now approaching…	40
Apprentice	42
Making My Shirts	44
Grandmother's Garden	45
Twenty-two Over Seven (or something close to it)	46
Frank…	49
The Room Beyond	50
The Permanent Way	52

A Kind of Alchemy	53
Two Postcards from Penzance	54
Somewhere Close to Hades	56

III

Sticky Fingers	59
38 Wetherby Road	60
Sharpenhoe Clappers	61
The Pink Bicycle	62
Weather Sonnet with a Stolen First Line	63
Like Willow-Pattern	64
The Photo of Sue at Jenny Lake	65
A Pound of Flesh	66
The Digital Version	67

IV

A. F. L.	70
Palm Springs	71
Big Sur Café	72
Caloosa	73
Midnight in Michigan	74
Life on the Road to Santa Fe	75
Cowboy	76
Natchez Trace	77
The White Car	78
Last Days	80

I

A poet is the most unpoetical of anything in existence, because he has no identity – he is continually informing and filling some other body.

(John Keats – letter to R. Woodhouse, 27 October 1818)

First Draft

This morning I've been bidden to write a poem about
an imagined person who might be me
if I weren't who I am.

It's basically the same old question
that we ask children – *What do you want
to be when you grow up?* – posed fifty years too late
and in a different tense.

I'm getting this sense of a tall, athletic individual
of Scandinavian appearance: firm, not-unpleasant features;
fair hair; and the sort of keen blue eyes
that would have been the first – of many pairs
in the long-ship – to spy (as it lifted
above the horizon) the stretch of foreign coast where,
one day, Scarborough might be.

With those well-formed lower limbs he would,
inevitably, be a consistent wearer of *le maillot jaune*
and his arms look as if they could effortlessly
straight-drive sixes into the stand at the Nursery End.

Yet he has the slim, sensitive fingers of a musician
which caress strings and stroke keys
with equal facility; he knows the name of every plant;
he is at one with stone
as it responds to the edge of his chisel.

By a strange co-incidence he has the same
wife as I. He wants so much to write lyrically of his love
for her but would be the first to admit that,
blessed as he may be, he is *not* a poet.

It is with great sadness, therefore, that I'm
reluctantly obliged to cross him out – and start again...

Wet Day at Lumb Bank

(for Julian Turner)

What had been fine drizzle – unfalling rain – has gained weight,
has lost its grip on air and clatters on leaves, on the tall
daisies hanging their heads by the iron railings, white petals
still returning light that everything else absorbs.

The hills are hunched, huddled flank-to-flank
under the grey of a sluggish sky, pressed close like sheep that shelter
in the lee of dry-stone walls; from somewhere beyond sight
the knock and drone of a passing train is funnelled up the valley.

On the lawn a poet frets his way through a cigarette, fair hair
and shoulders dampening; in the woods the birds continue
their communications unperturbed; the river mutters, concentrates
on wearing stone and – like his poem – grows a little… a little more.

Conjurors

(for Paul Hyland)

It's the way they use wrist, hand, fingers: those
liquid movements peculiarly theirs;
that flick and flourish like fish in a shoal
changing direction simultaneously,
flowing arpeggios you can't not-look at
while elsewhere the other hand slyly makes
some un-noticed move, retrieves or conceals
coins, cards, or that watch they're about to smash
inside the hanky you also lent them.
They will distract with motion, deceive you
smiling, rob you of breath, of certainty.

It's like poets: what they can do with words.
You know you can't trust them either, their sleights
of language, sudden shifts of attention;
how they build illusions out of meaning
and the mutability of meaning, make
uncertain everything you thought you knew.
Few are not showmen in some way – and you're
seduced, become a willing volunteer
stepping forward to lend them your belief,
hoping that when each trick's over, something
will have appeared. Or disappeared. Or changed.

Stubble-burning

All day he has waited for the wind to be right;
now, at dusk, flame runs behind him
as he draws out a line across the shorn field –
fire-hounds are off the leash, chasing the drag.

Air heats to visibility, a jagged orange wave
sweeps down the slope, the far hedge
shimmers. Black smoke fattens, flattens, flings
an offering of grey ash to the rising moon.

Along the moving rim heat consummates
the union of fuel and oxygen; in a nave of flame
dry stems spit and crackle-out their wordless
responses; the fire speaks only in tongues.

A Hurrying Stranger

Banishing mirrors from his own house
had been the easy bit – but he soon developed a habit
of avoiding the homes of friends
in which he knew he'd have to confront himself.

With time it became easier to find excuses
for not visiting, or for meeting somewhere else; he began
to draw his curtains early, before shrinking daylight
darkened the panes, threw back the lighted interior.

Walking near lakes and ponds was now reserved
for windier days when their choppy surfaces
fragmented any reflections – annoying, but not too
difficult to arrange. Shopping, though, was hazardous:

all those acres of plate glass at a variety of angles;
the *poseurs* flaunting mirrored shades; too many
over-polished cars. So, in town, he walked
head-down, mostly, though he noticed the camera crew

that lunchtime on the street but didn't bother
to cross over to avoid two grey-suited, grey-chinned
politicians being interviewed. Seeing them again
that evening on the television, he recalled

a small gathering on the pavement, cables he'd
almost tripped over, yet totally failed to recognise –
passing in the background – a hurrying stranger,
head inclined, wearing a jacket uncannily like his own.

Present Tense, Future Imperfect

If you believe that tea-leaves
or spirals of apple peel, fallen at random,
can foretell a future, then look
inside this black bag; but they will tell you less
than the chaos of cold pasta
tinged with tomato, the milk carton
weeping its last drops,
the empty chocolate box.

Notice how petals have scattered
from a disarray of flowers, once bunched,
broken stems cranked across an empty bottle;
then find, still deeper, moist with coffee grounds
and barbed with splintered picture-glass,
the globe of tightly-crumpled paper,
blue ink of cursive letters cracked into angles
on the note that said he'd gone.

Time and Place

The map shows an old aerodrome a few
miles to the north – that must have been the one –
and the shoreline's as he described it; so
is the village. Is this quaint or what? His claim

that it all looked a little like New England
is understandable: timber houses, small grey waves
tripping over themselves, and the grating sound
of shuffled pebbles are all familiar. It gives

her that craziest of ideas, the one of having been
here before – as if knowledge of a place
could be inherited – and, standing in the lane
outside the closed-up pub, she can share space,

though not time, with a fresh-faced GI in his swank
new officer's uniform and an adoring Suffolk girl,
sees a brief slice of light and hears the clink
of glasses and snatches of Glenn Miller that fall

out of the opening door. She watches the young couple
leaving, arm in arm, and follows up the track
past that tall, weird house. By the windmill
they light cigarettes, laugh as he tucks the pack

into her coat-front, then gently make each other dumb
with kisses. From across *The Meare* half-a-dozen geese
give raucous calls, strain into the air and climb
ponderously, like overloaded bombers, heading east.

Telephone Man

He crouches between the open doors
of a green cabinet on the pavement;
his hands progress as if reading Braille,
feeling up and down the columns
of tightly-coiled wires that bear
the important, the trivial, the amorous
and the angry within their striped bunches.

Then, like a hairdresser, he deftly twists
and snips the curls; as he pokes and preens,
a thousand conversations skim
under his fingers. The traffic ignores him
but, for a few seconds, I'm a voyeur
of his unsuspected intimacy, my mind making
connections, furiously dialling numbers.

A Sudden Surfeit of Squirrels

Moving like water – or, at least, as water would
if it could run uphill – they flow across grass,
up trunks, along branches, arc like fountain-jets
between twig-ends which shouldn't, by rights, be able
to take their weight yet seem so casually to absorb
every take-off and landing and still bob back again.

Grey as dusk, even in full sun they are half-light,
half-seen, indefinite when moving. The blurred edge
of departure – when you're left wondering if you really
saw anything at all or whether it was the wind, hurrying
through grass or starting that *Mexican Wave* among
the leaves – this is their party piece, their best illusion.

With an eye for the main chance and a perpetual need
to be elsewhere, they have recently moved in
from a neighbouring town like a gang of pickpockets
descending on a race-meeting; we see them daily,
at full tilt along the ridged capping of the garden wall
or gathered on Windmill Hill to inspect their spoils.

Approach, and they disperse like street traders – the way
the man who does the three-card-trick on an upturned
suitcase melts away when the police come round –
and they become fluid once again, a soft bow-wave
rippling out, only subsiding to stillness
somewhere beyond the limit of the eye's resolution.

Every Cloud

When the first Boeing came in through the wall
one floor below his office,
as luck would have it he'd earlier stepped out
(omitting to say anything to anyone) for a low-fat
caramel latte and to see his lawyer
about the divorce he'd long been contemplating –
but hadn't yet mentioned to his wife – leaving
an empty chair behind. So it was easily assumed
he'd only gone to the men's room,
which is what a colleague told his spouse when she
phoned some time after his departure and exactly
twelve minutes and seventeen seconds before –
outside a *Starbucks* and more than five blocks
away by now – he turned on hearing
the impact and explosions, saw that initial
flowering of flame, the morning sunlight skidding
off showers of glass mid-way to the ground.
In a dingy bar uptown he watched the TV play
and re-play the subsequent collision,
black pennants stretching out across the city,
then thirteen-hundred feet of tower
(including his desk and chair) dropping plumb
within the span of its own footprint and gone
in an exhalation of grey dust.
When he left, much later, it was dark,
the air's obscuring cargo still settling everywhere,
erasing his tracks as he walked north again.

A year later, he's watching ceremonies
on television. He's grown a beard. Where he's been
and what's happened in the twelve months since,
he's not talking about. He dips into

the flow of intonations, panning for familiar names
from his old firm, among them that guy who
came from Changewater, New Jersey –
whose wife's long had the life-assurance money –
but it's not *his* name any more
and, besides, he lives in Portland, Oregon, now.

Bug

I am a program bug, I lurk in software,
hide behind arrays, steal subroutines
and joyride the processor's mean streets.
Delinquent, data-molester, I am the bastard
of a tired programmer, unfaithful
to his wife, who – working late one night – took
no precautions, sowed a wild oat in a line
of program code.

Survival was hard at first but I
soon learned, during the purges, how to fool
the Systems-test Police, remained inactive.
Even when they questioned me I gave
all the right answers. Brimming with
streetwisdom now, I lie low in trashcans mostly,
judging the best time to come out
for a byte.

I am immortal though I lack theology,
die each time you power-down the chips
yet live on; am resurrected when
the program's run again (or not, depending
how I feel). Have I a philosophy? Oh yes:
I exist, therefore I frustrate – my aim in life
to leave you wondering just what
you did wrong!

Skylark

So much sound from a brown speck
mounting a column of sky:

it's the bubble of a spring – of water
hurrying through stones – that spills

over the slow drowse of the afternoon,
the chafing of insects in long grass,

and falls in a cascade to where we
lean on bikes, still listening effortlessly

when eyes strain to find
that only fleck of sky that isn't blue.

Glider

A reluctant dog, stretching the lead taut,
it lags behind the tow-plane
clambering through the tiers of air
over Dunstable Down.

When unleashed it pauses, pivots, puts out
a wingtip like a steadying hand
to regain balance, then grabs a thermal,
treads an unseen high-wire round

a tight helix, teetering higher, never quite
falling off. At last it spills
willingly from the edge of rising heat,
dives at the speed of a kestrel's

plunge on to prey, only to change its mind,
flick upwards, clawing height
from dwindling lift as momentum falters.
The pilot surfs sky, afloat

on the hill's updraught and the wind
curving over sculpted fibreglass
until, drawn irresistibly to ground,
he approaches the field; but above the grass

his craft hesitates, stays buoyant, clings
briefly to those last few feet of altitude, loath
to be re-joined to its shadow, become
inanimate once more on the earth.

Dawn by Numbers

(for Christopher and Marisa North)

Always at about four a wind comes,
riffles the *jalousies*, testing
our resolve to sleep on.
When church clocks chime at five and six,
the cock across the valley answers
with a few tentative crows.
At seven, the farthest mountains
which, last night, gathered round at dusk,
step back again; by now the rooster's
crowing steadily, convinced
that only by his exertions can the sun
he's just hauled over the horizon
be hoisted higher still.

Wall of Death

It was simply a matter of speed: he knew
that all he needed was just enough
to hold him up, to keep the tyres
sucking at the polished boards;
there was a kind of high in having the ability
to defy external forces, create
his own, to swing the bike up from the pit
and keep the blur of faces streaming past.

It seemed so easy: throttle open,
the saddle held him firmly as he watched
the curving wood slide into place
beneath him; now the wall swooped down ahead,
reared-up behind, became a revolving drum
that spun the wheels, left him stationary
on an endless hill he never seemed to climb,
forever at the foot and heading nowhere fast.

Not quite what he'd forseen, this shifted
perspective, this paradox of speed and stasis;
dependent on motion now and trapped
in the tight circumference, he began to sense
lightness becoming weight, like a stalled wing
losing lift, a flung pebble cresting
its parabola, or a man beneath a tangling
parachute: in freefall, and running out of sky.

Nocturne – Aldeburgh Beach

It's dark, now – and colder – and the sea's
sharp intakes and smooth exhalations
send sighs along the beach.
Yet they're still here, doctors
checking the ocean's slow breathing,
monitoring its heart through those rods,
their lines that dip and pull taut, dip
and pull taut with the water's heave and fall.
All afternoon they've ignored
a wind that builds height into the swell,
have listened to the gravelly cough
of the backwash, examined
sputum the shivering sea expectorates
at their feet. Now others join them, hang up
hurricane-lamps, bivouac in tents of light;
crouched on stools they'll stay
all night, keeping watch
with the dedication of anxious relatives.
And when the sound of wave
collapsing beneath wave has ceased teasing
our dreams, we'll see them
from our window in the grey before dawn,
quietly leaving the now-sleeping patient
who must have rallied with the tide's turn.

The Devil's Apprentice

And if you asked me what I used to do, I'd claim
    that I was once a Magician

who conjured motion from the four elements,
    nurtured air and flame to free the power of water;

who trailed the smell of sulphur in his wake,
    and studied a small black book of incantations;

who seared flesh in the furnace – and swigged
    a milkless brew, cold, from an old bottle;

who raced with time towards tomorrow's dawn,
    interrupting dreams with distant thunder;

who commanded fire to dance and flung sparks
    like tortured souls into the night sky.

Job Application

Dear Mr Barnum,

                I wish to apply
for a post with your organization. Although
not having worked in the industry before,
I feel that I'm well-qualified.

I've had plenty of experience of going round
in circles and of dealing with clowns;
clearing up huge smelly heaps left by others
has been one of my regular tasks.

I have learned how to keep many balls
in the air simultaneously – and how to smile
and maintain my equilibrium while others
are climbing on to my shoulders.

I'm familiar too with essential techniques
needed for keeping my extremities intact
when in the lions' den and know
how to avoid blowbacks when playing with fire.

Lastly, I'm used to treading a thin line
at altitude and also to remaining unsupported
for seemingly endless periods while
trying to meet a constantly-moving target.

I'm now looking for an opportunity to stand
at the centre of the ring and crack
the whip myself for a change. Should I
run away, come by train, or just roll up ?

Please write soon…

The man on Crewe station

watches departing trains
unpick the silver tangle of rails;
he notices the slow binary of tail-lights
as coaches wag through pointwork:
right then left; yes and no; wrong or right?

He has handed in the mobile phone,
the pager, the keys to the red Peugeot;
in the Admin. Office he handed in his life
to the girl with green finger-nails
who'll file and forget.

What started here is finishing here – he
could never have predicted that
nearly thirty years ago – and yet he's sure
he was never precisely *here*
before, not where he finds himself now.

There were nights far away – in trains,
on stations, tramping the length
of snow-covered yards, sliced by a north wind
that pummelled windows in the cabin –
when he'd wondered where the journey

was taking him. Like the model engine
in a train-set he has chased
down tracks, round curves, been stopped
by signals, shunted into sidings, but thought
he was generally headed somewhere

only to find that *somewhere* is back here.
Last night he dined with colleagues
round the table; this morning,

in a hotel lobby, the circle closed and he
was left outside. It has all the inevitability

of a film ratcheting towards its final scene,
the actor caught in tight close-up
behind rising credits. And should the camera
pull back at any time during the six minutes
he waits here for the train home,

place him in context, frame him
on the platform among this swelling crowd,
no matter how wide the angle,
the lens would always find him –
for those six minutes – utterly alone.

II

. . . the past falls open anywhere –

(Michael Donaghy: *Black Ice and Rain*)

Late Honeymoon

In my father's photo,
a black-and-white print he made himself,
the mountain hut is a silhouette
against a wall of rock where sky should be.
He says he took it back in nineteen-forty-nine,
that the tumble of ice across the valley,
just off-centre in the frame, is the glacier
below Mont Blanc, and that the female figure,
approaching through long grass – seemingly
an Alpine milkmaid – is in fact my mother
returning from a quick pee behind the cabin.
He claims that this was my first trip abroad:
I am there too, I've been assured,
but – so far – am not even a slight bulge.

"We are now approaching...

...Bristol Parkway, where we shall arrive shortly...

The railway here cuts contours
and, in the sixty seconds that it takes a slowing train
to get from the cutting's end at Penny Bridge
to the abrupt rise of Stoke Lane,
a segment of almost-familiar landscape swivels below,

reveals a place where becoming older
wasn't some kind of problem to be faced, more like
an edge-of-seat adventure, an Eagle comic-strip
or a radio serial in which we always longed
to know what would happen next.

For one minute the changing angles
of stone walls, hedges, slopes and valleys to the south
alternately display and conceal lanes,
rivers, woods, buildings, present and past
like some conjuror's sleight-of-hand.

It's a neat trick – this confusing
of place and time – but I've learned how it's done:
I know who once delivered Sunday papers
to that village; who almost fell
out of one of those trees one Summer holiday;

who annually won the sack-race at the hospital fête
held in that field over there (the one you can't
quite see any longer); who filled
his wellies trying to wade across that river;
who used to flatten pennies on this railway line.

There was Here and there was Elsewhere – which
was anywhere that wasn't Here or ours –
though if we thought we owned the place, then
we were wrong: it owned us, was reluctant to let go,
clung for a while, but eventually forgot...

*...and, when leaving, please make sure you take
all your personal baggage with you."*

Apprentice

On days when the sun shone he would net,
like butterflies, selected specimens
of life as they flitted past and pin them
to film; the whole world was struggling to get

inside his camera, it seemed. He stored
the negatives in old tobacco tins, safe
from damp and creasing, the delicate wafers
of cloudy monochrome hard,

if not impossible, to replace: baby portraits;
steam trains; the snow of '63; everywhere
we'd ever been on our holidays. It was all there,
waiting for the blacks and whites

to be reversed, made solid. He'd set out
in the darkroom three enamel trays – one
of the mystic numbers – pour in potions
from brown glass bottles, then douse the light;

and in the red glow from the safety-lamp his face
would resemble a poster for a horror film,
while I must have looked the same to him
as he focussed the image, cropped it to his precise

requirements under the enlarger, composed
his print. Only when fully satisfied would he take
bromide paper from a yellow, black-
lined envelope, lay it down to be exposed.

As it floated in the developer, at first
nothing seemed to happen; then darker streaks
would emerge from the blank sheet,
unidentifiable to start with, just

random shapes, thickening areas of grey
which deepened, spread, linked up, became
faces I knew, a hay-field and mountains
in Tyrol, or a boy in a cap and gaberdine the day

school first claimed him. I watched the ceremony
performed many times yet never tired of it,
willingly apprenticed in this black art
for which no other word exists but... *sorcery.*

Making My Shirts

After the ritual of the measuring-tape
she'd next translate my modest dimensions
into patterns, then a pile of cut cloth,
each piece the size and shape
of some part of me I couldn't quite recognize.
The *Singer* looked, to a child's eyes,
like a small, black pig standing on a table,
snout nodding as she flexed
her ankles on the flapping treadle,
slid grey *Clydella* under its enamelled belly.

I'd watch the steady travel of thread
from bobbin to needle to seam punched
through the fabric, listen to the mechanism's
smooth thumps, the ticks tumbling
one after another like a frenzied clock
as woven layers were stitched, pulled close,
and locked to my contours. Then, pins in mouth,
she'd slip it round me, the settling softness
warm, its lifeless two dimensions
drawing their first breath, swelling into three.

Grandmother's Garden

Close to the pond, where goldfish
dodged my shadow in the green water
as I trailed hands bloody from gooseberry bushes,
grew poppies, their petals more silk than silk;

the same flowers whose blaze once broke
through the mangled fields of northern France.
It was, of course, his garden too
but, having missed him by a couple of years,

I always thought of it as hers –
and hers only – though I'd held the medal,
fingered the rainbow ribbon he got
for turning up at Kitchener's invitation

and, each November, without comprehension,
had stood silent in tall, high-windowed classrooms
with nothing to remember, wearing
a sad, red imitation in memory of the others.

I saw old men who could have been his brothers
parading stiffly in red coats today –
and thought of him for the first time in years,
wondering what of him I had inherited

and if he would have been there if he could
or if, like me, he'd find such show
increasingly ironic, sigh, and mutter:
Silly buggers – don't they know?

Twenty-two Over Seven
(or something close to it)

(for Peter – who was there)

I no longer remember exactly whose
idea it was – mine or his – it was just one of those
things boys did in stories we'd read
(in the sort of books and comics that our parents
actually approved of!). Unbelievable? Not if
you re-calibrate for the mid-twentieth-century,
before safety-paranoia and faster trains:
we're talking *steam* here – noisy and, more important,
relatively slow – not certain death approaching
at two-miles-a-minute without any tattoo
of wheels on rail-joints to warn you; we're also
talking pennies an inch or more across, money with
a bit of metal in it, weight and worth –
solidity that'd buy a pack of Beech Nut, Wrigley's
or P. K. out of a machine (with that extra packet free
every fourth turn) – not those piddling little things
they fobbed us off with back in '71.

Fourpence: four pence – probably all we had
between us that day – plus a curiosity so strong
that we were willing to forgo what they'd have bought
in Trebor chews, Holland's *Penny Arrows*
or Fry's chocolate in the interests of experiment.
So, having watched a goods train labouring
much-too-slowly past, we descended to the track
to find, in close-up, everything much larger
than expected: the sleepers deep, their cracked bulk
sweating creosote into stone chippings,
some as big as our fists; the polished rail-heads
broader than our coins and slightly convex.
With not a little urgency we laid

four pennies along the nearest rail, retreated
high up the cutting's side, and waited...

I think it was an up South Wales express,
Castle Class loco working hard against the gradient,
eighty-inch driving wheels slowly stealing speed
from the drag of fourteen coaches, each
of those massive wheels a metal-press on the move,
squeezing with a force of over ten tons:
it came at us across the long embankment,
snorting like the dragons in fairy tales that we
already considered ourselves too old for,
roared hollowly on the bridge, and stamped
on our precious currency. And though, I'd swear,
we stayed focussed on the exact spot,
we saw nothing happen as locomotive, tender,
carriages rolled across our coins.

With the tail-light hardly past us and the rails
still singing as the last coach swayed
eastwards towards London, we were back.
Two remained lying where we'd left them; one
had dropped between the stones; all three
now enlarged, but thinner with knife-sharp edges,
oddly distorted, oval, and slightly curved
like the railhead where they'd lain.
Still warm, they shone as if newly-minted.
The fourth we never found although we searched
fifty yards of track before we noticed,
imprinted on the surface of the rail, something
not unlike a royal seal, a monarch's head and motto,
but in reverse, repeated every twenty-one feet
or so, starting clear, then fading until
it became almost a shadow – then invisible.

Our first thoughts, I recall, were not about
what might have happened to it
but the regularity of that mark, how it recurred
at even intervals: once, we realized, every
revolution of the wheel. And although too young
to have learned that mathematical formula of *pi*,
here, at least, was a demonstration of it
that we understood – though at a cost:
for the penny was gone and, saddened by our loss,
I don't think we particularly cared
whether it would adhere just long enough to be
flung off at some far junction or if our copper
had been forged into intimacy with the steel tread
and gone forever looping down the line.
But neither, at that age, were we able
to foresee the cutter's torch creeping closer –
and all of this, so soon, becoming history.

Frank...

(i.m. Frank James Godfrey, 1883–1948)

...your name, lodged between my other two,
remains unused – unless I'm filling-in
official forms – another part of you
that came to me. Sitting here at a screen
addressing lines to you, I'm conscious that
you too assembled words (though not your own)
with monotype machines, and speculate
on whether you'd think the skill's gone
from your craft. Had you survived a few
years longer, in retirement you'd have met
the grandson who now writes this and who,
this once, includes your name below. Type-set,
it's snug between my other two and, though
we never knew each other, dares me to forget.

John Frank Godfrey

The Room Beyond

It hung on the chimney-breast
above the all-night stove, the circular gilt frame
patterned in relief, the glass convex
so that the room beyond it was
our dining-room but also – somehow – not.

The furniture was all in there:
the carpet the same rust-brown island on green lino
but its geography was subtly changed –
as was the table's – edges curving
like long bays out to headlands at the corners;

and the curtains bowed just like the table-legs,
matching a suggestion of drunkenness
in the door and window frames. In that other room
another family – not unlike us – lived,
apparently unaware that we were watching.

Through there, the routine was much like ours:
each morning Father riddled the grate,
took out a pan of pale ash, put on
a few shovelfuls of anthracite, then opened-up
the damper; and I suspected that their stove, too,

roared streams of flame that curled
up and over the back-boiler and hurled themselves
into the chimney. But no matter how close
I managed to get my eye to the glass, this theory
stayed unproven – every time, a leering,

distorted face would block my view. Unless
we ate in the kitchen, the others could always
be seen to have their meals when we did;
and their children went to the same schools,
though both my sister and I are certain we never

saw them there – except, maybe, in class photos.
It's just an old couple by themselves now,
their offspring visiting occasionally.
When their grey-haired son took a picture,
I could see my wife, smiling over his shoulder.

The Permanent Way

Down here, things move more slowly than they did
the last time we came this way
with steam tumbling, wheels hammering on rail-joints,
the dry flutter of wind snatching at open windows,
and sudden views – always too brief – cut off
by stabs of stonework or a rush of sloped grass
rolling as we passed. Once, when ten, I asked
the Driver of the 5.13 if he could go more slowly –
and he laughed and flew the three miles
out to Fishponds in a dash that left us breathless.

Now, with the track gone, we walk cuttings
and embankments, beneath bridges, and notice how
a railway imprints its surroundings – sometimes subtly
in the sculpting of land, sometimes forcefully
with structures built to last: each individual blue brick
precisely placed in the curve of an arch
making the whole as solid as Victorians
who were certain *this* was the future. We look out
across rooftops that used to circle in formation
or up at the bottoms of gardens, the ends of streets.

"That," my father says, "is the house where I was born."
We take a photo, joke that it ought to have a plaque,
then turn, and amble back, trying to separate
what's changed from what's imperfectly remembered.
Up on the road again, drowned by the blare of traffic,
we look over a bridge parapet: along the bank
tall grasses lean in unison – as if swept by the wake
of something slipping past; not a slow freight,
struggling and spitting sparks, but a long express,
its lighted windows flickering in the night.

A Kind of Alchemy

As the year expanded into summer, so
the tough wood of elder forced, out of green,
the gentle cream of petals opening with the sun.

We picked the heads for wine, desecrated
their pale softness,
let water and sugar leach their essences.

Now time and yeasts have plaitted in
the cool cellar, lace blooms upon the tongue;
we sip gold – the taste of another day.

Two Postcards from Penzance

Morning: the flag on the Queen's Hotel stands stiff
In an off-shore breeze; the Promenade railings throw a graph

On to the pavement; a cart heads for Newlyn. Puffed sleeve
To puffed sleeve, their full skirts touching, two women who give

Every impression of not being in a hurry stroll
Away from the camera, joined paper-doll to paper-doll.

The tide is in, tight to the sea wall and, just now, all
That might be safely predicted here is that, soon, it will pull

Back to stroke the beach, fold frills at its edge; there's little
Else that's certain, only the pebbles' intermittent rattle.

To her friend in Leatherhead, Miss Charmau,
M.L.W. wrote: *July 11th, 1902. The cabman brought us here,*
a very nice boarding-house right on the Front
and our bedrooms both look out over the sea. We are off
by coach to Land's End. Hope you are still improving.

If I've judged distances and angles right, I'm standing
Precisely where the tripod stood while, bending

Under a black cloth, the photographer dragged the scene
Into focus, an inverted image on a ground-glass screen

Glowing in his small darkness. Then, for that moment,
The day looked in on the exposed plate and its silent

Glance imprinted two women, a cart, a flag, this Promenade,
These railings, that hotel and the same sea on silver iodide

But noted nothing remarkable on a morning when the only thing
Of consequence was that a man with a camera came.

*April 9th, 1999. We walked up from the station; we're staying in
an old house right beside the church and our room here
looks out over the sea. Trying to take a photo of the Front
but am having problems with the light and perspective. I'm off
by bus to St Ives. Hope the weather starts improving.*

Somewhere Close to Hades

(for JBD with thanks for an enjoyable afternoon near Redruth)

The building imitates its materials: masculine,
square and true as the granite blocks piled precisely;
only the chimney allows the frivolity of curves,
only the slant of a gabled roof deviates.

So what really amazes is the grace with which
nine tons of cast iron repeatedly measure
their exact arc of sky, translate
the piston's push and plunge into rotation.

It's eighty years since the engine's suck and swash,
the hollow cough of steam exhaled,
the minuet of rods and cranks and flywheel
last raised – from three-hundred fathoms below –

ore hand-hewn by candle-light in a region
somewhere close to Hades; yet it dances delicately on,
an old lady remembering the steps, if not the music,
the ball, if not the chandeliered ballroom.

Turning the car we pause between reverse and forward,
notice our alignment with the winding-drums,
calculate aerial angles: directly beneath us
the capped shaft descends, descends, descends. . .

III

Sue poems

Sticky Fingers

Each time I hear it, night
rushes towards me on the A64,
the old Viva's struggling
to make sixty, laying a smoke screen,
and Mick and the boys
are whumping it out:
Brown sugar...!
Great music to watch
your petrol-gauge fall by –
but the price is up again,
fifty-five bloody pence per gallon
and they say it'll be
over a pound by Christmas.

The route to you was measured-out
in tracks from that album,
it being the only tape I owned:
always *Wild Horses* drawing me
past Copmanthorpe; *Bitch*
riffed from one end of Tadcaster
to the other; *I Got the Blues*
at Bramham crossroads;
Sister Morphine crossing the A1;
then a delivery of *Dead Flowers*;
and by the outskirts of Leeds
they'd be telling me you were
   *... just another Moonlight Mile
on down the road.*

Can't You Hear Me Knocking?

38 Wetherby Road

It existed because it filled a need:
Novello Villa – we couldn't have invented it –
a theatrical boarding-house
with an ever-changing cast of characters,
new every week. Or fortnight.

Whoever was on at *The Grand*, they all
stayed there. Sometimes you'll recall
half of The Royal Ballet crowding
your top-floor flat to watch a Royal Wedding
(you had the only television in the place);
the Scots comedian who washed
his Rolls-Royce out the back;
the ageing leading-lady who advised you
in her well-known, throaty tones to "Wear red,
darling!" on your first day as a teacher…

But *I'll* be remembering your single bed
with the Grand Canyon running up the middle,
where we had to sleep back-to-back
to stop ourselves falling in.

Sharpenhoe Clappers

Late March, our anniversary,
and of all days this to be grey:
sky, beech-bark, the grey mingling
of soil and chalk in fields
scraped by the plough
gives yet no spit of green;
only in the torn hedges
are there flecks of growth
and in the continuity of wide
grass stretching behind us.

Up here the grey wind
takes colour from the landscape,
swishes the beech-clump,
snaggle-toothed from storms;
where fingers of root
still grasp a few inches of earth,
a cold hand reaches
for a butterfly; the severed
trunks show rings, count time.

Sharpenhoe Clappers is an area of beech woodland on the edge of the Chiltern Hills which was donated to the National Trust in memory of two brothers killed in the First World War.

The Pink Bicycle

If the girl on the pink bicycle and her following father
hadn't been riding their machines on the pavement
there'd have been no performance (at the pedestrian crossing)
of the small dance of confusion watched by a bus-driver
delayed on his schedule, inevitably wondering
with growing frustration precisely how many of
these bloody idiots were, in reality, going to cross

for it turned out that his wife (no, not the bus-driver's),
who'd totally mis-read her husband's intentions,
was herself – by now – crossing while he, with no need to,
shook his head at the driver and watched her receding
as he stood there kiss-less (as, indeed, *she* was)
which was not how he'd meant this particular parting –
pre-arranged though it might have been – to happen at all

but led to the thought that her untimely departure
might prove to have robbed him (or her, for that matter)
in the event of disaster in the near future, whether
train-crash or lightning-strike (but excluding earthquake
for madness lay that way), of a last osculation
which – although not entirely – is *why* he'd been hoping,
as was his custom, to kiss her goodbye

yet in this endeavour had failed completely
owing to the absence of her keys from the kitchen
and her search of their bedroom after he'd kept *her* waiting
for over ten minutes; which explains (in some measure)
why it was that the pair of them, the pink-bicycle rider,
her father, the bus, and twenty-nine passengers
all co-incided – and his wife went unkissed.

Weather Sonnet with a Stolen First Line

Shall I compare thee to a Summer's day?
Perhaps – but not the one we had last week
when rain slung out of a murderous sky
crackled like small-arms fire, spread a sudden lake

across our street, and every brilliant spike
grounded far too close for comfort. Though now
I come to think of it, maybe it's like
the night that we first met. You're wondering how?

Well, I know it didn't rain, there was no wind,
no thunder and no lightning; yet I felt
I'd been engulfed by a small storm – the kind
that's alive with static – I got quite a jolt

from somewhere. Not lightning, though, no blue arc
sizzled; *you* hit me with a smaller, gentler spark.

Like Willow-Pattern

It had maybe come from a market somewhere;
a stop-gap, stand-in, one of two – short-term
replacements for those they'd packed in boxes,
shifted down from Leeds in a hired *Transit*

(among all her worldly goods she'd recently
endowed him with) and buried in a stack
in his parents' garage. A very English scene:
church, churchyard, lych-gate, thatched cottages,

and a village pond; blue on white like
willow-pattern – but not – chunky earthenware
they drank every cup of tea and coffee from
during those eight weeks in the bed-sit

up Cheltenham Road and, after he'd copped-out
of carrying his almost-new bride across
the threshold of their flat in Clifton, the first
few mugfuls as they got themselves unpacked.

One was soon broken, but this cracked survivor
she's today displaced from holding brushes,
toothpaste, dental-floss, stayed unseen for years
just by being there. So only now

does he notice how it's aged – cheap glaze
faulted like limestone, crazed in less time than
they've been married – and find that tiny willow,
trailing long, blue branches in the water.

The Photo of Sue at Jenny Lake

Arranged upon a boulder, knees drawn up
in mermaid pose, you're laughing – probably
at something stupid I'd just said – it's
the Summer we took a boat across the lake
below the Tetons, hiked the rocky trail
up through the woods… until you lost a heel
and had to hobble slowly down again,
one leg slightly shorter than the other.
But that was later; now I find my camera
caught not just your laugh, the *Laura Ashley*
trousers you wore out last year, a tee-shirt
I don't remember but, there, down near
the bottom edge, your right boot – the heel
already starting to become detached.

A Pound of Flesh

(selected scenes from the movie of the same name)

No gentle rain from heaven but a clear blue sky, just as in
Manhattan three mornings earlier; the same feeling of unreality,
too, and that sensation of being felled, of also having been
on the trajectory of something not seen coming.

That's scene one, in which they're returning homewards
on a country lane – not much dialogue here – and everything
outside the car so visibly unchanged, conspiring to be
just the same as usual, so unrepentantly normal.

In the second scene our heroine – for it is she – is on
a trolley being wheeled down a long white corridor while he
watches in silence, a bit-part player for the moment,
wishing the bloody director would cut that swelling music.

There's nudity in scene three – essential to the plot – and she
accepted this when pitched into the part. She's in the bath;
a glimpse of fading scars, left side, inner quadrant:
in truth, less than a pound – but still closest to the heart.

The Digital Version

In the hedges they can't stop talking
about the wind: in advance of each gust reaching us
a rumour goes round the trees
which lean towards each other, pass it on
in a whisper that rises to a mutter, then becomes a shout
before they straighten from their huddle
like guilty schoolgirls surprised by the ensuing silence.

Above Noon Hill a Red Kite holds its space on the sky,
taming air that lurches in from Bedfordshire
as if drunk, stumbling over the Chiltern edge to fall
on us without apology. Below, some tiny animal,
which hasn't noticed the sickle wings
or the rusty blur that now descends like a meteorite,
will stay content, if hungry, for less than a second longer.

Her camera is counting colours, calculating
a million degrees of green beneath a blue that shades
continuously from the sky's crown to the horizon;
it all pours in through the lens, cross-stitching with light
the points where that bird was, is, will be
in a moment's time – though within *this* frame
an anonymous small creature may yet scutter away.

IV

O my America! my new-found land . . .

(John Donne: *Elegie XIX*)

A. F. L.

(American as a Foreign Language)

We're back – and the traffic moving
fender-to-fender on the freeway lets us know
we've not been missed.

We're back on the beltway, the turnpike,
the highway, making lefts, hanging rights,
and turning on red;

avoiding citations for traffic violations,
yielding at intersections,
having a nice day;

we're back in the boondocks, on dirt roads,
on blacktops, lodging in motels
with faucets that drip.

We're back where vests and pants are rarely white
and men wear suspenders openly
without fear of embarrassment;

where biscuits and muffins still take us by surprise,
buns always come in pairs, and twenty fags
is nearly half a busload;

we're back where adjectives, nouns, and verbs
are having some kind of identity crisis,
prepositions bulge from every phrase,

and the adverb is a seriously endangered species.
No Sir, we ain't vacationing – we're back
to learn the language.

Palm Springs

*. . . moth-blurr of blades against the light,
generating fire out of air.*

Gillian Clarke: The Wind Park

At first there's just a single row
high on a brown hilltop, a line
of trefoil blades chopping the horizon.
Further on they fill the valley floor,
planted in groves: steel fronds tumble,
jostle, wired to the city
where, outside a hotel on Main Street,
parallel rows of tall palms flap green blades
in imitation. Indoors, behind glass walls,
the cycle of air–fire–air is completed:
ceiling-fans revolve, move lazily,
generate slight wind.

Big Sur Café

Take it all in: notice the way
the road you came on moulds itself to each
coastal indentation, rises, falls, but holds
a breathless height above the beach.

Recall the description; recognise
the grey, weathered planks, the loop of stairs
climbing to the deck, the paintings and bare pine
in the café, the waving firs.

Out on the verandah, talk to the girl
travelling north – your co-incidence as frail
as the paper parasol in her drink;
be certain that you won't forget her smile.

Take it all in: while you sit
with your coffee, five thousand miles from home,
consider how you were targetted here,
like an arrow, in search of a name

found in a newspaper, and reflect
on how easily an airline ticket and a map
can get you anywhere, located so precisely
despite distance. Then get up:

look out over low mist at the sky
stretching westwards; watch surf curl at the elision
of land with water – do you leave now, or later,
or simply delay decision?

Take it all in – and, before you set off, be aware
that, beyond the Pacific, further than you
have already come, the land resumes,
goes on. Take *that* in too.

Caloosa

It is said that the Caloosa, a people of
the Everglades before the Spaniards came,
believed that Man has three spirits:

the first lived in the shadows
that sprang out of their feet,
went everywhere with them in the sun,
sometimes ahead,
sometimes behind,
often alongside as a companion, friend,
but always
moving when they moved,
halting when they paused,
and, at night, leaping back, frightened,
from the flames of their fires;

the second dwelt in the eyeball,
could look both inwards and outwards,
knew all their thoughts, saw
everything they saw;

and as they bent over water,
to drink or to spear a fish, there would be
the third, looking back at them,
to be raised in the hands when washing
and smoothed over the face each day.

Did you cup hands this morning,
catching the image on
the still surface in the basin,
lift water to your face?

Did you feel the perfect fit?

Midnight in Michigan

(for Carolyn)

Cicadas inflate the air to bursting;
lightning-bugs stab their sudden trails between
the trees; a freight train hoots for the crossing
down the road; and more stars than I've ever seen

at one time are splashed across a sky
by Jackson Pollock, a scatter of white
droplets flicked at black and stopped by the eye,
caught mid-way from brush to canvas, yet

all maintaining motion – except one:
following the familiar shape of *The Plough*,
I find the Pole Star lodged above your barn;
east, across a quarter of the world, it's now

five a.m. where the fir tree by our back gate
points towards that same, un-moving, light.

Life on the Road to Santa Fe

The highway south gives *straight* new meaning,
and nothing prepared you for this being
half way from somewhere to somewhere else
and so far from anywhere.

The last town was like all the others – a lurid
mile of burger-joints and motels – and that clown
in the big rig, leeching your rear fender,
pulled in for diesel and coffee way back.

Passing the first cactus your eyes flick
to the gas gauge, seeking reassurance, sweep
miles of sagebrush for other vehicles –

there are none; for now the future
is all telephone poles and yellow coneflowers
bobbing by the road and distant mountains
never getting any nearer.

But by afternoon you're in the mountains;
on the dirt-road a curl of red dust clings
like a bad reputation. After the third pass
the plain's heat reaches up once more

and, back amongst desert scrub and mesas,
the radio's talking Navajo and all you understand
is *Taco Bell* and *Kwik-Lube*.

It's late, and getting later, but the road
insists; the windshield's dusty now, you're almost
off the map; then, in low sun, the first adobe houses
melt out of a hillside – adobe, the colour

of earth, of dried blood, the colour of landscape –
while in the mirror, blacktop reels out behind
towards successive rows of mountains:
brown, then blue, then grey, then only sky.

Cowboy

He slots steers into the slatted maze:
a black-brown wave washes from side to side
along its alleys; the sum of hoofbeats
on packed earth is the roar of a river in flood.
Muscled backs swerve and eddy; pens
fill and empty like an irrigation system, the flow
diverted, held, released again at his bidding.
Little has changed here at the stockyards
in over a hundred years: denim-shirted,
tall astride his horse above the muck and stench
of ten thousand cattle, the bellowing
from as many throats, he pumps torrents of beef
down the channels. It's hydraulic:
from the catwalk we watch sixty head
impelled under our feet. He looks up, nods
and tips his Stetson to us as he passes – a gesture
less of now than of the eighteen-nineties –
although, this being the twenty-first century,
tonight he won't make camp, hitch his stallion
to a tree; he'll hook a horsebox on
his pick-up truck, drive home through city traffic.

Natchez Trace

Before steam, this was the way they returned:
Kaintucks, boatmen of the Tennessee, Ohio,
and Mississippi Rivers on a one-way trip
with the current; who sold their cargoes,
broke-up their rafts for lumber, then foot-slogged
hundreds of miles back to Tupelo,
Nashville, or beyond to do it over again.
Along this forest trail tramped men who rarely
got rich: in the small townships that grew up

to meet these travellers' needs, the cost
of food and lodging, whiskey, and the money
they'd lose at poker all gnawed at the profits;
but, if they avoided being robbed along the way,
there was just a chance they'd come out
better than break-even. Then stern-wheelers
began to ply the rivers – working upstream
as well as down – and *The Trace* was obsolete.
Towns emptied; it took less than twenty years.

At Rocky Springs the chapel still holds
monthly services but, around it, building-timbers
have rotted to nothing and any stone or brick's
been carted-off long since. All they left
was a pair of bank-safes – walls of solid iron
lined with concrete – too heavy to drag away
and probably useless, keys gone missing.
Rusty doors gape among the pines; shelves
are slowly being stacked with wind-blown soil.

Rocky Springs, MS.
Population – 1860 : 2,616. Population – 2000 : zero.

The White Car

You know how it is: you're reading Billy Collins
at a quarter-to-two in the morning,
lying in bed at The Gibson Inn, Apalachicola, Florida
(not just because you only bought the book
the previous morning but because
it's *that* sort of place: easy – Ginger on the desk
said there are no rules here – and, besides,
you're so far from anywhere else that matters
it makes you feel it's quite OK to do this if you want to...)

and you're contemplating turning out the light
when some clown overcooks it on that tricky little left-hander
coming off the bridge-ramp on US 98

and his tyres start yelling – of course, you're familiar
with this old refrain that loosely translates as, "Oh, no!"
(and sometimes, also, "Not again!") –
then there's at least two metallic crunches followed
by a convincingly final thud

and, by the time you get to the window and part two slats
of the Venetian blind, there's already
a squad-car pulling up, disco-ing blue and red,
then a second, a third, a fourth
(in a town *this* size, for God's sake?)
like they need to reach some sort of critical mass
before anything else can happen;

and now the whole street's
strobing like a dance-hall and the clown in the white car
that has crossed the sidewalk and is steaming gently
on the forecourt of the beauty-salon opposite
isn't the usual clown but a slim girl
in jeans and a pale green tee-shirt who has got out and

is leaning against the side of the white car –
which, very surprisingly and from your viewpoint at least,
is showing no visible damage – while the cops
(who have multiplied like fruit-flies) swarm round
making measurements, looking underneath
the white car and doing all the sorts of things
cops do in these situations
but which they alone understand

and, while the girl in jeans and a pale green tee-shirt,
arms extended sideways, palms turned up, jabs
at the air with her fingertips as she appears to remonstrate
with two of the officers, all the time
there's this big black dog
(which may – or may not – have anything to do with it)
hanging round, lurking, circling in
and out of the shadows, watching… just watching…

and, after you let drop the cocked slat and go back to bed,
you hear the towing-truck arrive,
which not only adds a further colour to the thin beams
lasering across the ceiling but also mixes in
an audio track of engines revving and a sound that might
be the girl in jeans and a pale green tee-shirt crying
or could be metal scraping across the road
(but is, in any case, the last thing you remember);

and, in the morning, the street's empty,
wiped clean like a blackboard:
no cops, no lights, no girl, and, particularly, no white car
or black dog, just two orange cones
at the edge of the sidewalk by a hole where
something used to be: a fire hydrant,
a stop-sign, or a lamp-post? But *that* you can't recall.

Last Days

Once more the point's been reached
from which all routes are homewards,
and you're driving on the levée,
welded to the steely green-grey
of the Sacramento River above low farmland,
high sun unmoving in a thin sky,
burnt grass and walnut groves,
yellow and green fanning past;

and it's not because you're bored
with the radio's FM rock or tired of the rhythm
of telephone poles, or even because
it's lunchtime (that's just an excuse)
but you turn across the bridge,
head for the little diner on the other bank,
where the men gather after fishing,
and it's coffee and banana cream pie,
Just once more.

It's then you realise that you've
been here before – not here precisely,
not in location but in time –
so many times that time paused long enough
for you to tie another knot into the rope
before it slipped again.

And it's always the waiting you remember,
never the departure: each knot anticipates
the blankness of rope running through the fingers,
ties you to a place and time
when something was about to end –
and you're no longer here
but on a station platform, in an airport bar,
loading the last tea-chest on the van,
or, as a child, watching icicles drip, knowing
that tomorrow the last snow will be gone.